THINGS THAT SPIN

From Tops to Atoms

Books by Irving and Ruth Adler

THINGS THAT SPIN: *From Tops to Atoms*
NUMBERS OLD AND NEW

Books by Irving Adler

SEEING THE EARTH FROM SPACE
HOT AND COLD
WEATHER IN YOUR LIFE
DUST
THE TOOLS OF SCIENCE
THE SUN AND ITS FAMILY
MAN-MADE MOONS
MONKEY BUSINESS: *Hoaxes in the Name of Science*
HOW LIFE BEGAN
MAGIC HOUSE OF NUMBERS
THE STARS: *Stepping Stones Into Space*
TOOLS IN YOUR LIFE
FIRE IN YOUR LIFE
TIME IN YOUR LIFE
THE SECRET OF LIGHT

THINGS THAT SPIN

From Tops to Atoms

by Irving and Ruth Adler

The John Day Company New York

To spin a top, first you wind a string around the top. You hold the free end of the string between your fingers. Then you throw the top to the ground. At the same time, you pull the string away from the top. As the top falls, the string unwinds. The unwinding string makes the top spin. The top stands up on its tip, like a dancer on her toes. It spins and spins for a long time.

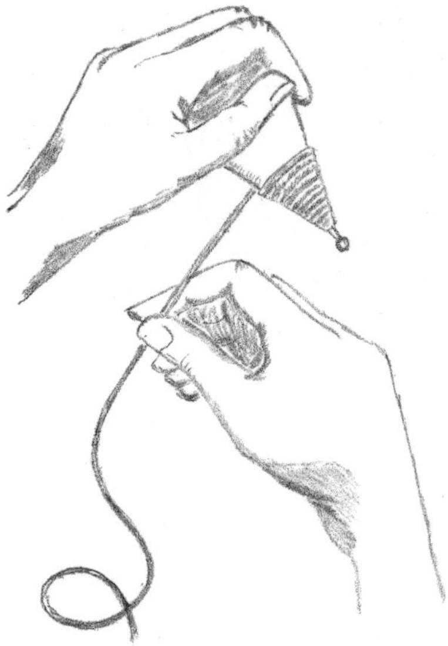

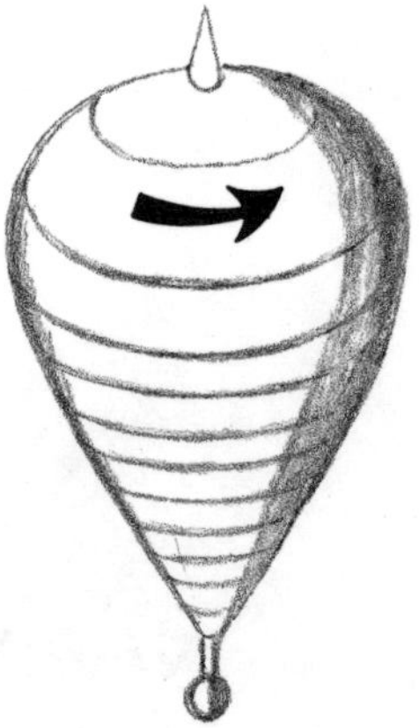

There are many things in the world that spin like a top. Some of them are found in nature. Others are made by men to do useful work for them. There are spinning tops in the sky. There is a spinning top under our feet. There are spinning tops in some machines. In fact, there are spinning tops in

Library of Congress Catalogue Card Number: 60-10265
Manufactured in the United States of America

every thing we look at. But they are so small that we cannot see them. This book will tell you about some of these tops.

While you are playing with a toy top, you can learn from it, too. By watching it as it spins, you can find out what spinning tops can do. This will help you understand many things you see in nature and in machines.

You spin a top by pulling the string that is wound around it. The string gives the top one big turn, and makes it go round and round. Once the top begins to spin, it keeps on spinning for a long time. It stops spinning only when something stops it. If you touch it, it slows down and stops. Even if you do not touch it, it slows down and stops after a while. This is because something else touches it. The ground touches the bottom of the top. The air around the top touches it all over. The ground and the air both rub against the top as it spins. This rubbing is called *friction*. The friction

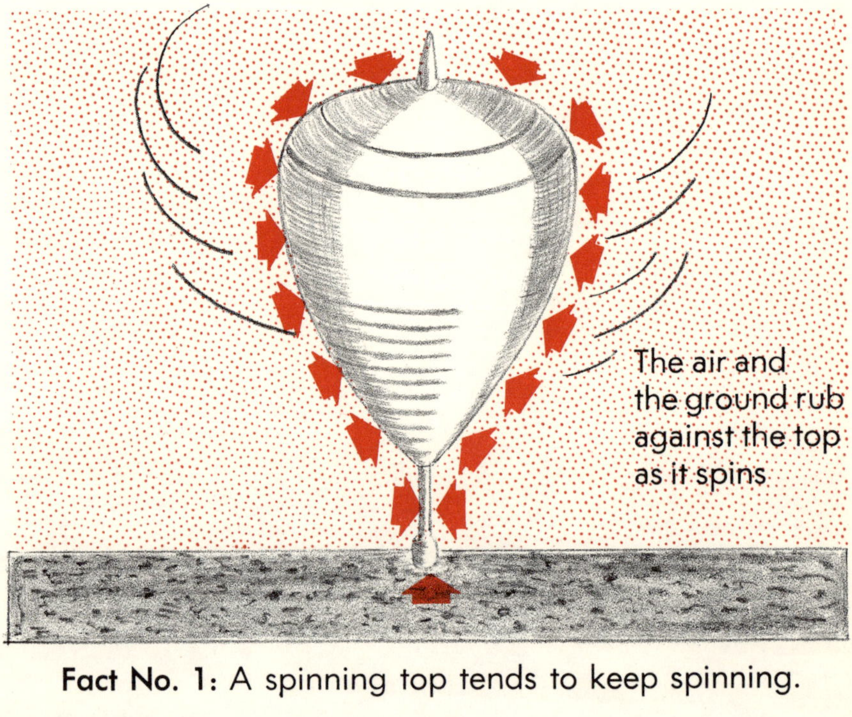
The air and
the ground rub
against the top
as it spins

Fact No. 1: A spinning top tends to keep spinning.

makes the top slow down and stop. If there were no friction, the top would spin forever. This is an important fact about tops: *A spinning top keeps spinning.* Let us call this *fact number one* about tops.

When a top spins, there is a line through the middle of the top around which it spins. This line is called its *axis.* If the top starts spinning with its axis standing up straight, it stays that way for a long time. Unless something else pulls it, *the axis of the spinning top keeps pointing in the same direction.* We shall call this *fact number two* about tops.

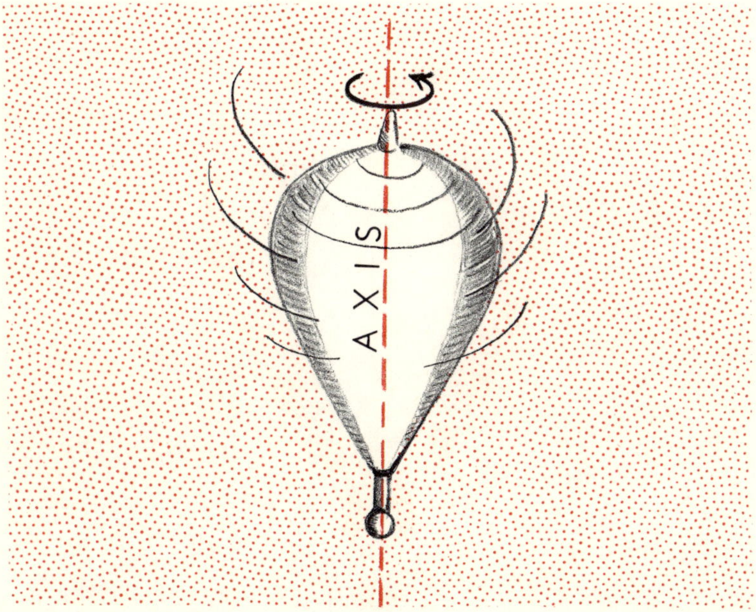

Fact No. 2: Unless something else pulls it, the axis of a spinning top keeps pointing in the same direction.

In toy stores, you can buy a metal top made of a wheel and axle. The axle is mounted in a frame made of two rings. The frame can stand still while the wheel spins. Two legs are attached to the frame in line with the axle. The end of one leg has a tiny cup-shaped hollow. The end of the other leg has a notch in it. With a top like this, it is easy to do a jug-

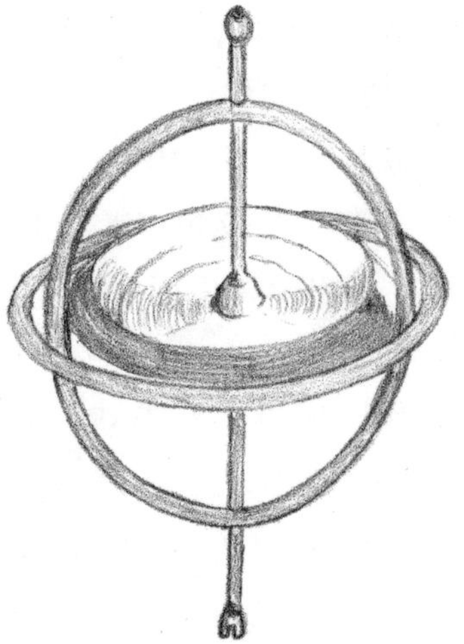

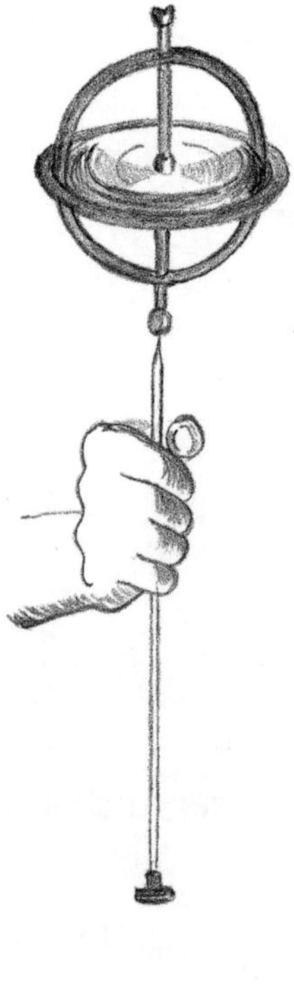

gler's balancing trick. Spin the top, and place the cup-shaped end of one of the legs on the point of a knitting needle. As long as the top spins, it will stand upright on the point of the needle. The top will stay upright, even if you tilt the needle. If the top is upside down, you can place the notched leg on a stretched string. Here, too, it will stand upright, without falling. Fact number two explains why this happens. The axis of the top keeps pointing in the same direction as long as the top spins. That is why it doesn't lean over and fall.

A top like this, made of a wheel and axle, is often called a *gyroscope*.

Without spinning it, rest a gyroscope top on the point of a knitting needle. Hold the top so that it leans over. Then let go. You will not be surprised to see the top fall to the ground. The weight of the top pulls it and makes it fall. Now try it again, while the top is spinning rapidly. This time you are in for a surprise. Even though the spinning top leans over, it does not fall. Instead, the axis of the top swings round and round. This swinging of the axis is called *precession*.

If the top is not spinning, it falls

If the top spins, it does not fall. It swings round and round.

The swinging of the axis is the result of a fight. The axis of the spinning top tries to stay where it is, pointing in the same direction all the time. But the weight of the top tugs at the axis and tries to pull it down. The axis holds back while the weight pulls. Neither one wins the fight. Instead, the axis swings, just as two boys tugging at each other may swing round and round. This is *fact number three* about spinning tops: *When a top spins, a force that pulls on the axis doesn't make it tip over. It makes it swing around instead.*

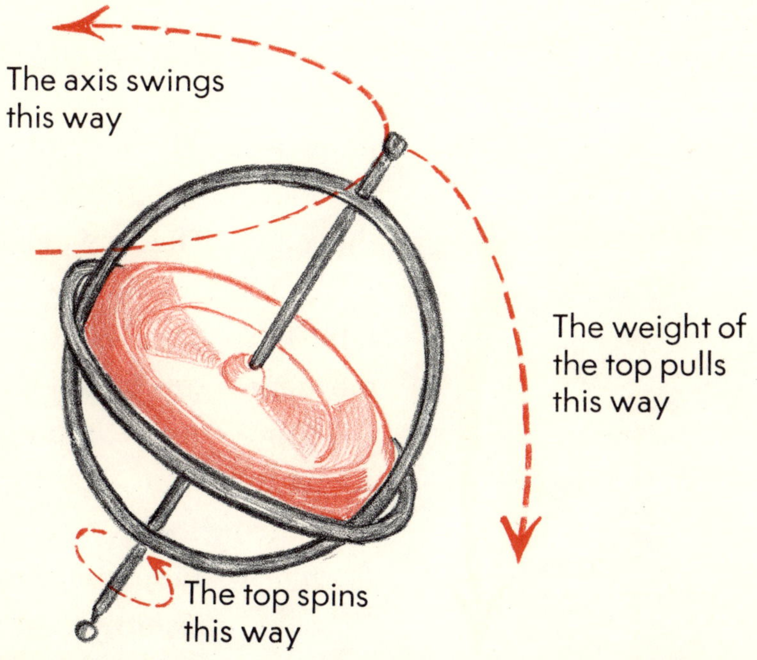
The axis swings
this way
The weight of
the top pulls
this way
The top spins
this way

Fact No. 3: When a top spins, a force that pulls on the axis doesn't make it tip over. It makes it swing around instead.

The turning wheel of a car is a spinning top. If the wheel is wet, it spatters water all around. The water on the wheel breaks up into drops. The drops shoot away from the wheel as if they were being pushed away from it. This push is called *centrifugal force,* or force driving things away from the center. To see this force in action in another place,

put a penny on the turntable of your phonograph, near the edge. Then switch on the 78 RPM speed. The turntable is like a top. As it spins, the penny shoots off, away from the center. It is pushed off by the centrifugal force.

We have found *fact number four* about spinning tops: *When a top spins, a centrifugal force pushes anything on it away from the axis.*

To find the next fact about spinning tops, we need a top that can shrink while it spins. You can make one with a piece of string. Tie one end of the string to a small weight. Hold the string with one hand, and begin swinging the weight around in a circle. The swinging weight is like a spinning top. You can make this top shrink by pulling the string in, between your fingers. The turning string becomes shorter, and the weight moves in closer to the center. When it moves in, the weight starts going around faster than it did before. This is *fact number five* about spinning tops: *If a spinning top shrinks in width, it begins to turn faster.*

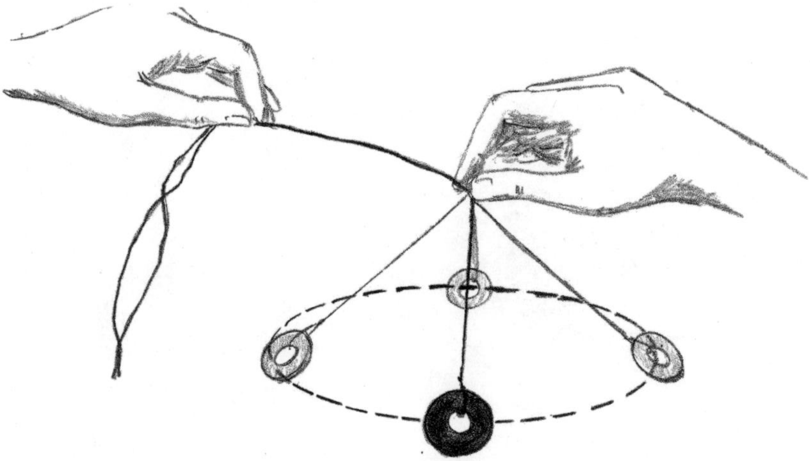

Fact No. 4: When a top spins, a centrifugal force pushes anything on it away from the axis.
Fact No. 5: If a spinning top shrinks in width, it begins to turn faster.

You can make a top out of yourself. Stand in the middle of a room, and start spinning around. Watch the walls of the room as you whirl around. They look as if they were turning around you, going the other way.

Sometimes you take a ride on a top. A merry-go-round is a large top that spins around. When you ride on a merry-go-round, it looks as though the ground is turning. These are examples of *fact number six* about spinning tops: *If you are on a spinning top, and look away from it, everything you see looks as though it were turning around you.*

The room seems to turn this way . . .
. . . when you turn this way

Fact No. 6: If you are on a spinning top, and look away from it, everything you see looks as though it were turning around you.

We have found six facts about spinning tops. Here they are in one list:

FACT NUMBER ONE:
A spinning top tends to keep spinning.

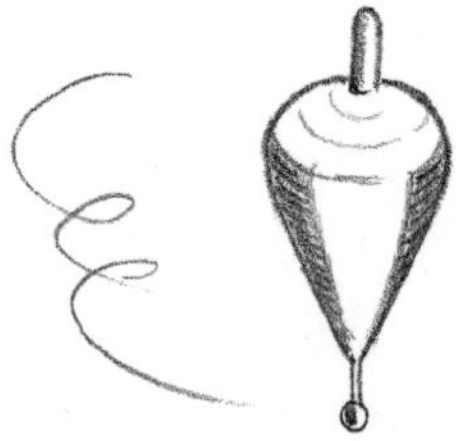

FACT NUMBER TWO:
Unless something else pulls it, the axis of a spinning top keeps pointing in the same direction.

FACT NUMBER THREE:
When a top spins, a force that pulls on the axis doesn't make it tip over. It makes it swing around instead.

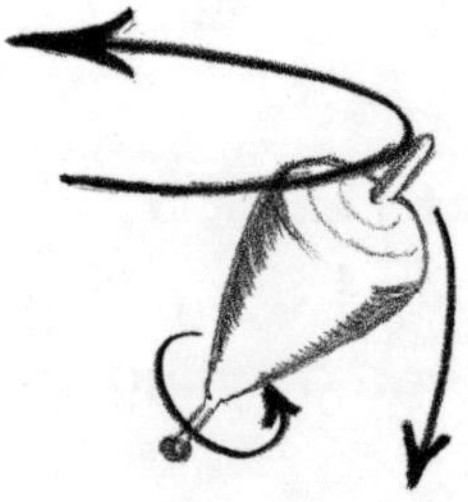

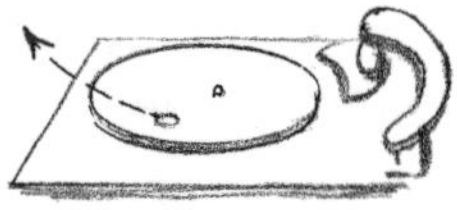

FACT NUMBER FOUR:
When a top spins, a centrifugal force pushes anything on it away from the axis.

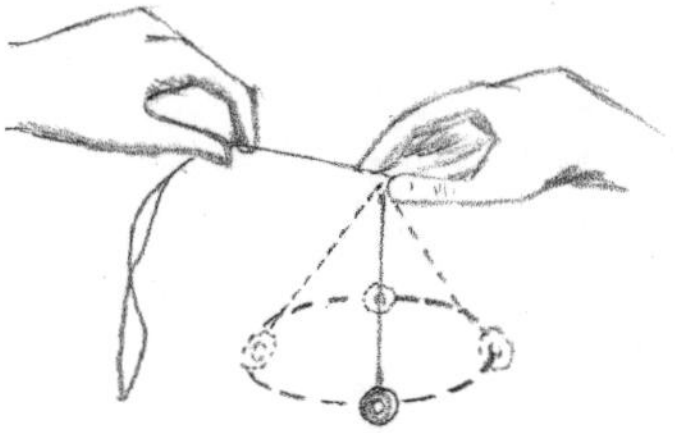

FACT NUMBER FIVE:
If a spinning top shrinks in width, it begins to turn faster.

FACT NUMBER SIX:
If you are on a spinning top, and look away from it, everything you see looks as though it were turning around you.

In the next pages we see how these facts explain many things that you may have wondered about.

When you ride a bicycle, you do not have to push the pedals all the time. After you get a good start, you can *coast*. Why does the bicycle keep moving while you coast? Fact number one gives you the answer to this question. The spinning wheels of your bicycle are like tops. They tend to keep on spinning until something stops them.

Fact number one is also the secret behind two popular toys, the yo-yo, and the spinning button.

The yo-yo is made of two wooden wheels mounted very close to each other on one axle. A string is attached to the axle in the narrow space between the wheels. To use the yo-yo, you wind the string around the axle. Then, while you hold the end of the string, drop the yo-yo. The string unwinds as the yo-yo falls. The unwinding string makes the yo-yo spin like a top. When the string is all unwound, the yo-yo does not stop. Because it is spinning, it begins to climb up the string, winding the string up on the axle again. Then it begins to fall again. You can keep the yo-yo moving up and down by moving your hand up and down in step with it.

You can make a spinning button yourself. Thread a long string through two holes of a large button. Tie the ends of the string together to make a loop. Hold the loop with both hands, and swing the button around until the string is wound up tightly. Now move your hands gently apart. As you stretch the string, it will unwind, and make the button spin. Then the spinning button will wind the string up again. If you move your hands gently in and out, you can keep the button spinning back and forth for a long time.

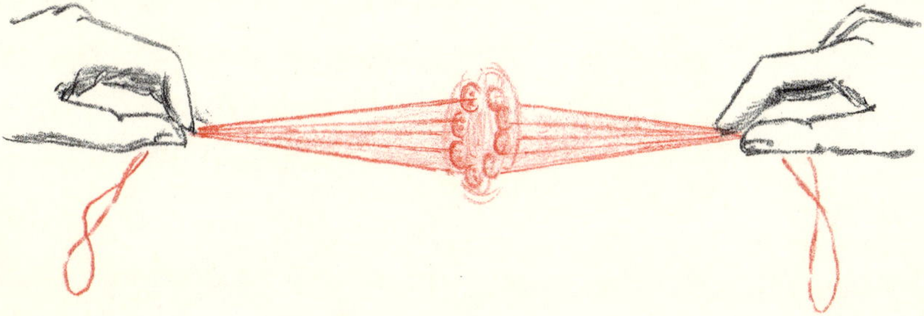

A standing bicycle will fall over if you let it go. But a moving bicycle does not fall. Why? This question is answered by fact number two. The turning wheels of the bicycle are like spinning tops. The axis of each wheel runs through its axle. The axis of a spinning top tries to keep pointing in the same direction. So each wheel behaves like a stubborn animal. It does not allow itself to be tilted. The axles stay level, and the bicycle does not fall.

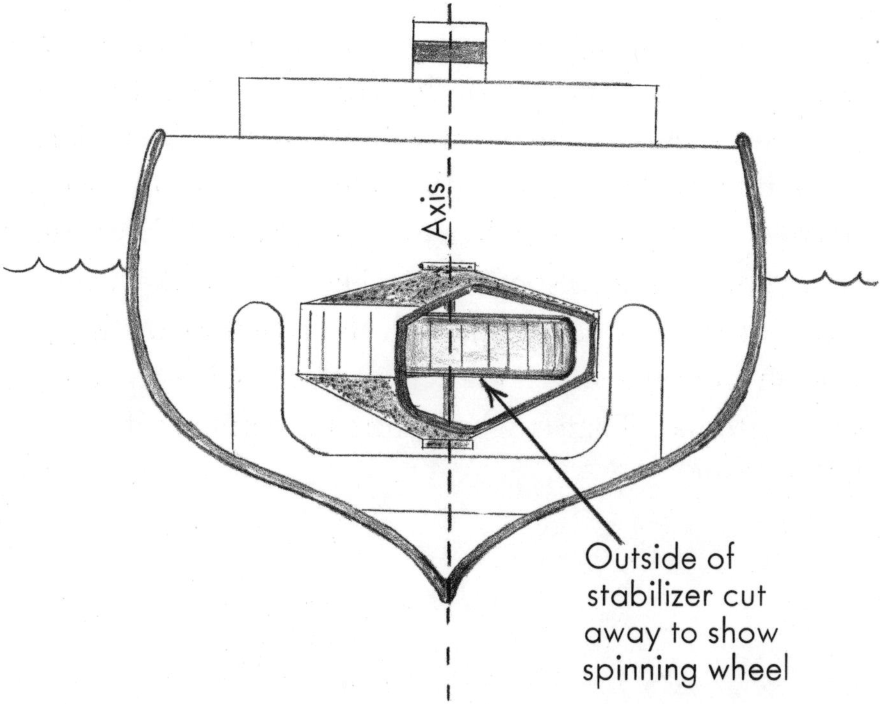

In sea-going ships, large spinning wheels (gyroscopes) are mounted for use as *stabilizers*. Their job is to keep the ship from rolling. When waves pass under the ship, they try to rock the ship back and forth. But rocking the ship would make the axis of the spinning wheels tilt over. The stubborn wheels do not allow this to happen. So the ship stands up straight in spite of the waves.

Gyroscopes are also used as stabilizers for airplanes. They form part of the instrument known as an *automatic pilot*. The automatic pilot can keep the plane flying level and straight.

Do you know how to make a rolling hoop turn a corner? To make it turn, you push it from the side at the top. This may seem strange the first time you do it. You might think that pushing it from the side will make the hoop fall over. But it doesn't fall over at all. Fact number three about spinning tops shows why. The hoop is like a spinning top. Its axis passes through the center of the hoop. A push from the side does not tilt it. It makes the hoop swing around. That is why it turns a corner instead of falling over.

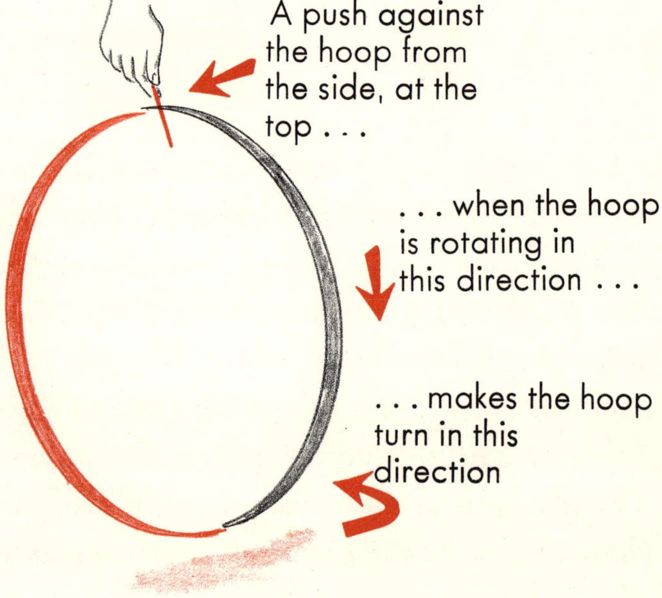

A push against the hoop from the side, at the top . . .
. . . when the hoop is rotating in this direction . . .
. . . makes the hoop turn in this direction

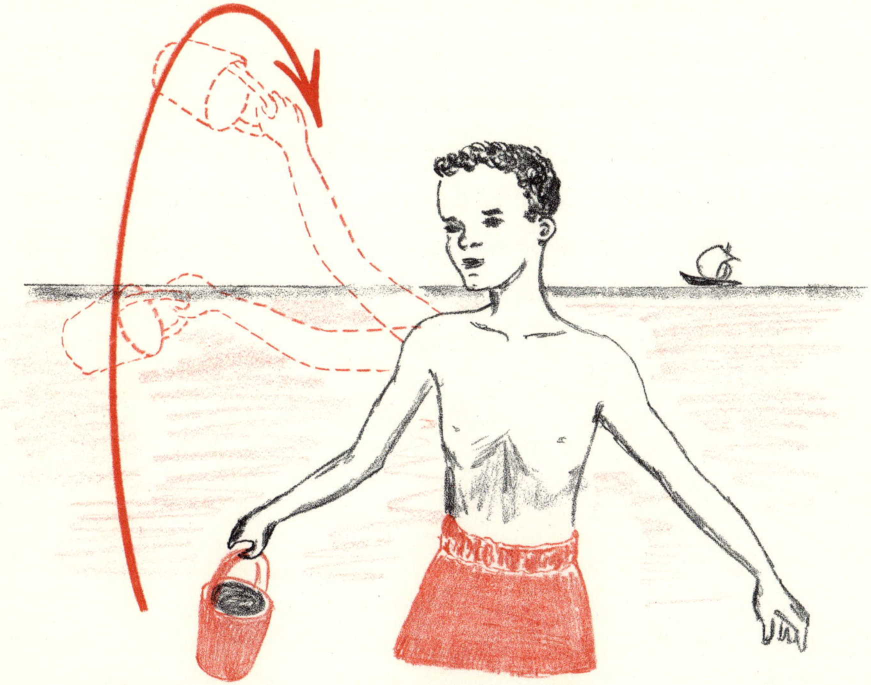

Can you turn a pail full of water upside down without spilling the water? You *can,* in this way. Hold the pail by the handle, with your arm straight. Then swing your arm around quickly. If you swing the pail fast enough, the water will not spill, even when the pail is upside down. Fact number four about spinning tops tells us why. As the pail swings around, a centrifugal force pushes the water away from your hand. When the pail is upside down, the force pushes the water *up.* So it keeps the water from falling *down.*

There are times when a centrifugal force pushes *you* so hard, it makes you lean over. This happens when you ride in a car, and the car goes around a curve. As the car rounds the curve, it moves along a circle, the way the outside of a spinning top does. The centrifugal force pushes from the center toward the outside of the circle. That is why, when the car rounds the curve, you lean over toward the outside of the curve.

People in the car
lean over in
this direction

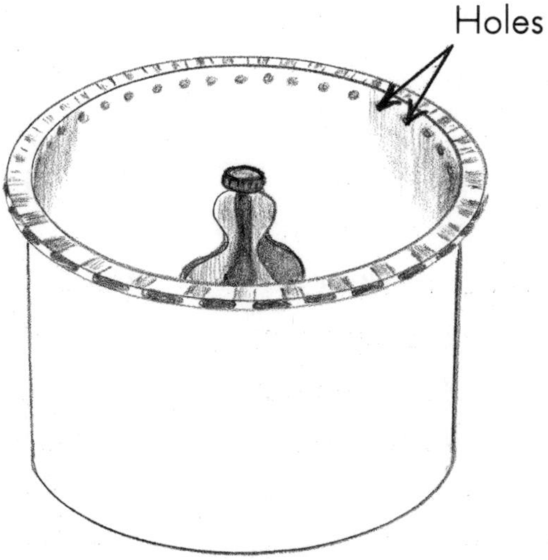

Drum of washing machine

There are many machines in which we put centrifugal force to work. In a *washing machine,* we use it to wring the water out of wet clothes. The clothes are in a large drum which is set spinning like a top. As the drum spins, the centrifugal force pushes the clothes against the side wall of the drum. The push squeezes the water out of the clothes. It forces the water up the wall toward the top of the drum. Near the top there are holes. When the water reaches the holes, the centrifugal force pushes it through the holes out of the drum.

A figure skater is a dancer on ice. She wears ice skates instead of slippers. But she does glides, leaps, and spins, like a dancer on a stage. It is interesting to watch a dancer or a figure skater do a spin. She begins spinning with her arms stretched out. Then she suddenly pulls in her arms close to her chest. When she pulls in her arms, something strange happens.

She begins spinning around faster! If she stretches out her arms again, she slows down. Fact number four about spinning tops helps us understand why this happens. The spinning dancer or skater is like a top. When she pulls in her arms, the top shrinks in width. But when a spinning top shrinks in width, it begins to spin faster.

A spinning dancer can control her speed by moving her arms in or out. We can control the speed of a turning engine in the same way. We put a set of metal arms called a *governor* on the shaft of the engine. When the engine spins, centrifugal force makes the arms swing out. The swinging arms stop any sudden changes in speed. If the engine suddenly goes faster, the arms go out further. But when the arms are further out, they make the engine slow down. If the engine suddenly slows down, the arms come in closer. But when the arms are in closer, they make the engine speed up. In this way, the governor keeps the speed of the engine steady.

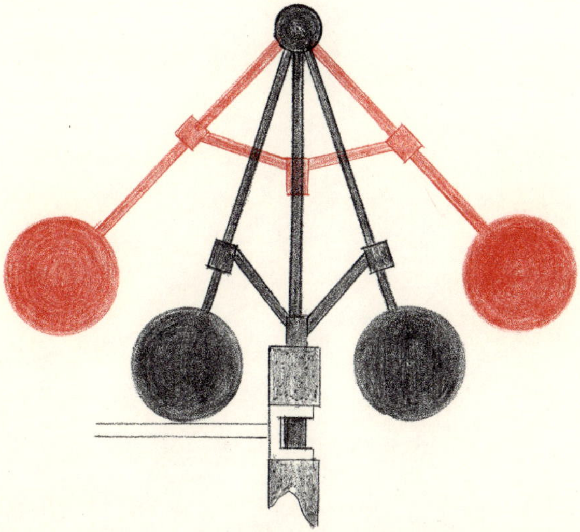

A governor. If the engine speeds up, the arms swing out.

There is a spinning top under our feet. It is the earth. The earth is a great ball that is spinning all the time. The axis around which it spins is a line that passes through the center of the earth. The ends of the axis are called *poles*. One is called the north pole, and the other is called the south pole. Half way between the poles there is a great circle around the earth called the *equator*.

If a person stands at the north pole, the ground spins around him like the turntable of a phonograph. But he doesn't see it spin, because he turns with the ground. To see the earth spin, he must compare it with something that does not turn. He can do this with the help of a

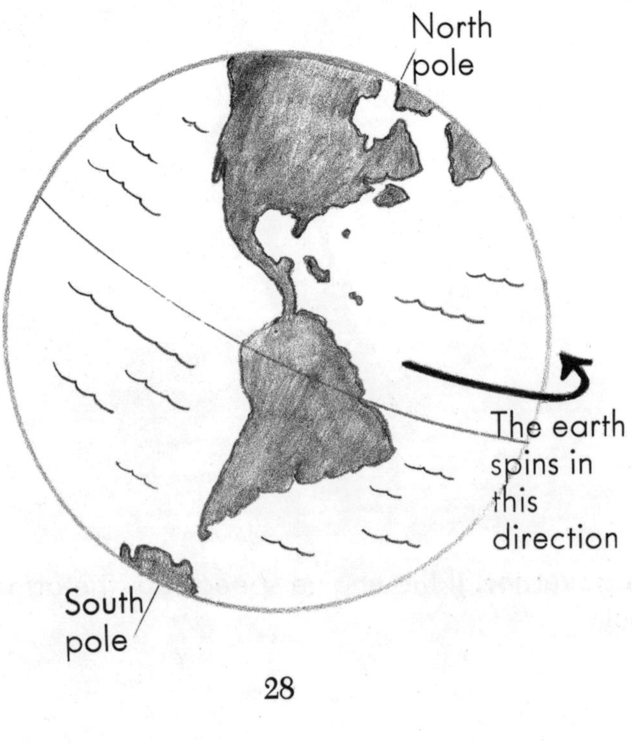

pendulum. A pendulum is a weight swinging at the end of a string or rod. *A swinging pendulum does not turn.* If a swinging pendulum is held over the north pole, the ground turns under it, from west to east. To a person who turns with the ground, it looks as though the pendulum turns the other way, from east to west. It makes a full turn in twenty-four hours. At places between the pole and the equator a swinging pendulum turns more slowly. There is a big swinging pendulum in the United Nations building in New York. As it turns, it proves to the visitors who watch it that the earth really spins like a top.

As you stand on the ground, you can swing around to face in many different directions. The direction toward the north pole is called *north.* The opposite direction is called *south.* Half way between north and south are the directions we call *east* and *west.* As the earth turns, each point on the ground except the poles goes around in a circle from west to east.

A captain of a ship at sea has to know which way is north so that he will know how to steer his ship. There are many ways of finding out which way is north. One of

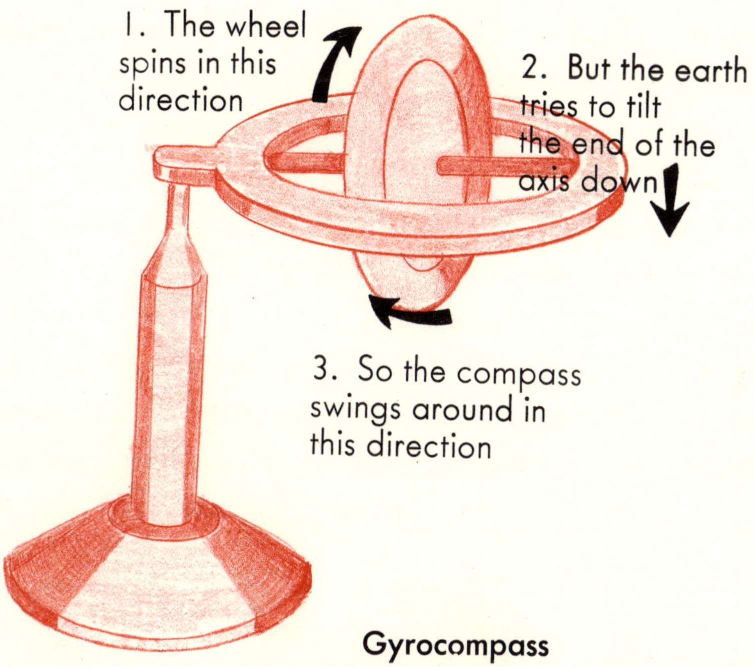

1. The wheel spins in this direction
2. But the earth tries to tilt the end of the axis down
3. So the compass swings around in this direction

Gyrocompass

them uses a spinning top called a *gyro-compass.* The gyro-compass is a spinning wheel that is mounted so that its axis is level, but is free to swing around. Suppose the axis points east and west. As the earth spins, it tries to tilt the east end of the axis down, and the west end of the axis up. But the axis of a spinning top will not tilt. It swings around instead. (Fact number three) So the gyro-compass swings around until its axis points north and south. Then it stays that way. No matter which way the gyro-compass points at first, it always ends up pointing north and south.

Every day is made up of two parts. There is daytime when it is light, and nighttime, when it is dark. Day follows night and night follows day. This happens because the earth spins like a top. The light of daytime comes from the sun. The sun is a large hot ball of gas. It is 93 million miles away from the earth. The light from the sun falls on one side of the earth. The light cannot pass through the earth, so it does not reach the other side. The space that sunlight does not reach is the earth's shadow. It is dark in the shadow. The side of the earth that faces the sun gets light from it. On that side it is

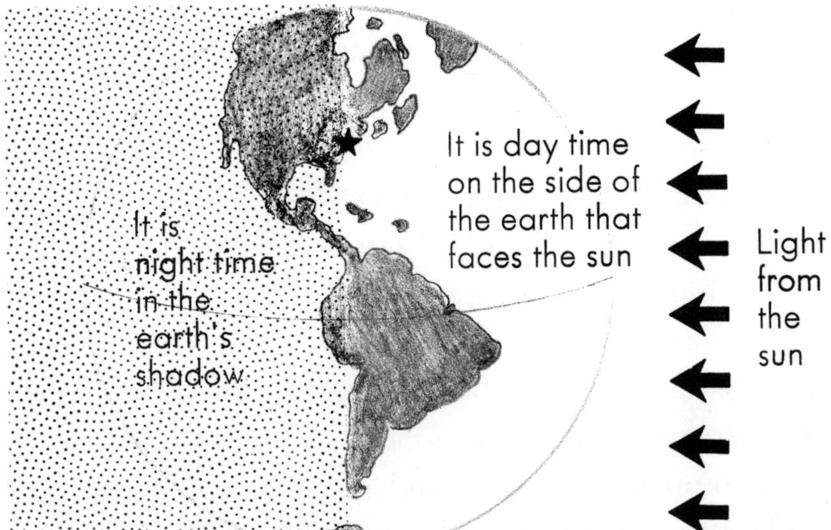
It is day time on the side of the earth that faces the sun
It is night time in the earth's shadow
Light from the sun

★ For someone who lives here, the picture on the next page shows how sunrise and sunset seem

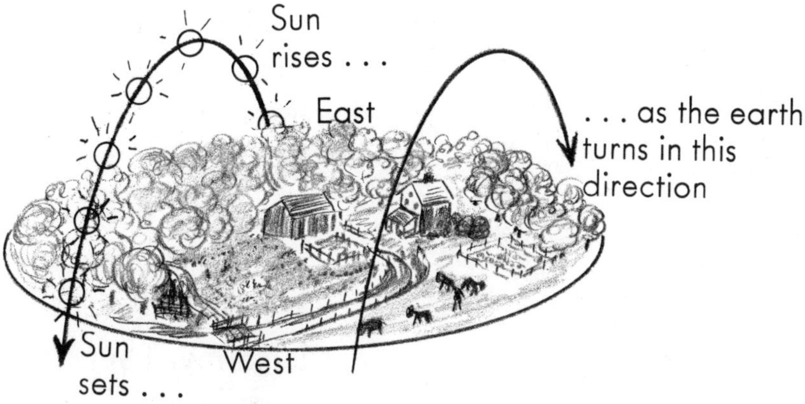

daytime. The side of the earth that is in the shadow gets no light. On that side it is nighttime. But the earth is spinning all the time. So the part of the earth that is in the light does not stay there forever. It turns around and enters the shadow. Then it turns around some more, to come out of the shadow and back into the light. In this way night follows day, and day follows night.

When you stand on a turning merry-go-round, everything around you seems to turn the other way. We are standing on the earth, and the earth turns like a merry-go-round. So everything around the earth seems to turn the other way. That is why it looks as though the sun moves in a circle around the earth. The earth turns from west to east. So the sun seems to go from east to west. It seems to rise in the east, pass over our heads, and then set in the west. We see the sun set when our part of the earth enters the earth's shadow.

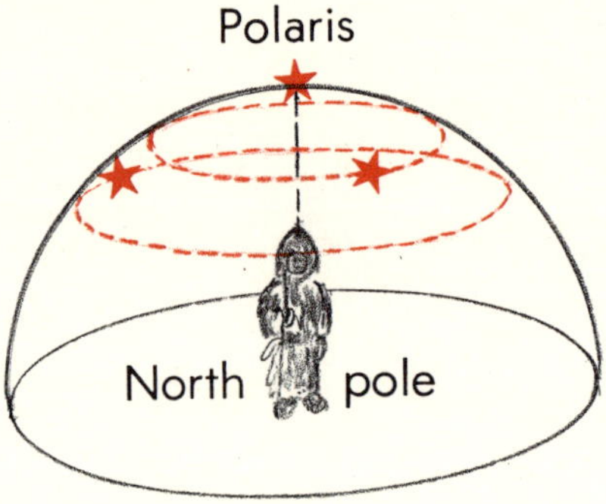

There are many, many large hot balls of gas like the sun. They are larger than the earth. They surround the earth on all sides. But all of them, except the sun, are so far away that they look tiny. They are the stars that we see at night. They look like small dots of light pasted on the inside of a big black bowl. Because the earth spins, it looks to us as if the sky were turning, carrying the stars around in circles.

The turning of the sky does not look the same from all parts of the earth. Up at the north pole the ground turns around like the turntable of a phonograph. A man standing at the north pole would see the star called *Polaris* (the North Star) right over his head. Because it is overhead, *Polaris* would not seem to move. But all the other stars would seem to move in circles around *Polaris*.

At the equator, the ground turns like the surface of a barrel rolling on the ground. There the stars seem to rise in the east, cross the sky together, and then set in the west.

At a place like New York or Chicago, between the north pole and the equator, *Polaris* is not overhead. It is

At a place like New York, Polaris is lower in the sky

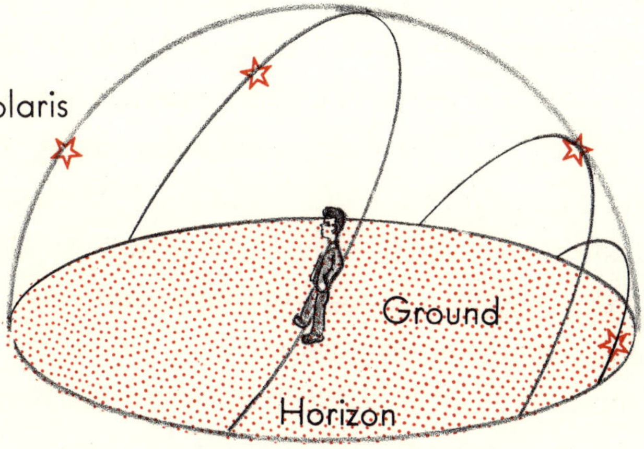

lower in the sky. Here, too, *Polaris* does not seem to move. But the other stars seem to move in circles around it. The stars that are seen near *Polaris* in the sky make small circles. They never set. Other stars that seem further away from *Polaris* make large circles that are partly hidden by the ground. These stars rise and set, the way the sun does. The stars furthest from *Polaris* in the sky make small circles that are completely hidden by the ground. People who live on the northern part of the earth never see them at all.

As the earth spins, it also moves through space. It moves in a big circle around the sun. The path of the earth around the sun is called its *orbit*. The earth makes a round trip around the sun in a year.

The sun is pulling on the earth all the time. This pull tries to make the earth move in toward the sun. But when the earth moves in its orbit around the sun, it is like a car going around a curve. So there is a centrifugal force pushing the earth away from the sun. The push opposes the pull. So, instead of falling into the sun, the earth just keeps swinging around it.

The moon is a big ball 240 thousand miles away from the earth. The moon travels in a circle around the earth

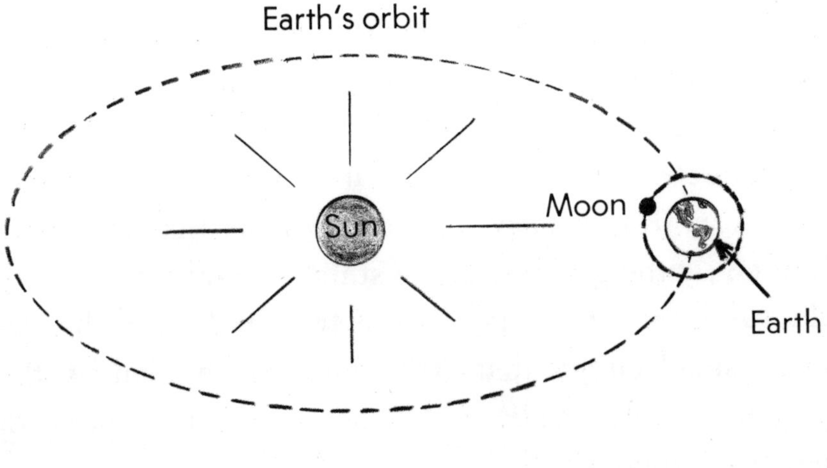

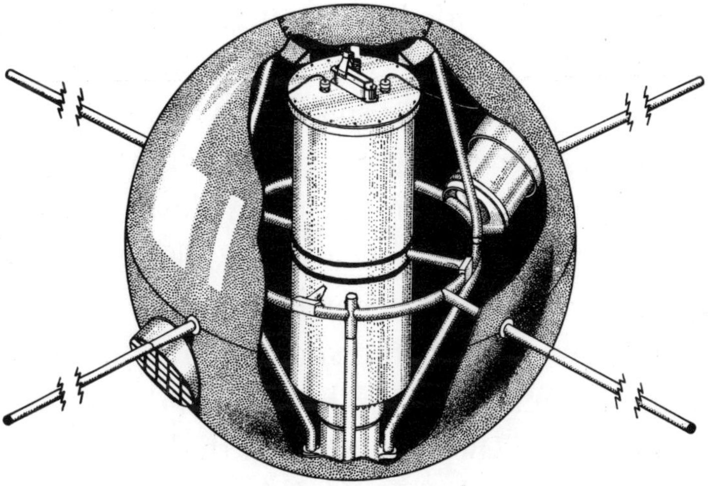

Adapted from U.S. Army Photograph

the way the earth moves around the sun. The weight of the moon tries to make it fall down to the earth. But, as the moon swings around the earth, a centrifugal force pushes it back. So it doesn't fall, but keeps moving around and around. The moon makes a round trip around the earth in a month.

A few hundred miles away from the earth there are some small bodies traveling around the earth the way the moon does. We call them *earth satellites*. They were thrown out into space from rockets fired by scientists of the United States and the Soviet Union. They do not fall right back, because centrifugal force holds them up. Most of them make a round trip around the earth in about an hour and a half.

Every year is divided into four seasons. First there is winter, when it is cold. Then there is spring, which has mild weather. Later, it is summer, when it is hot. Then comes the fall, when it grows cool. Then we have winter all over again. The four seasons follow each other in order every year. The facts we have learned about spinning tops help us understand why. The earth moves along its orbit around the sun. At the same time, the earth spins around its axis. The earth's orbit is like a road around the sun. The axis of the earth does not stand up straight on this road. It is tilted. It is always tilted in the same direction because it is the axis of a spinning top. The drawings on the next page show the earth at different places in its orbit. In the second drawing, the north pole is tilted toward the sun. The half of the earth that is north of the equator catches a lot of sunlight. It is summer there. Meanwhile, the south pole is tilted away from the sun. The half of the earth that is south of the equator catches only a small amount of sunlight. It is winter there. The third drawing shows where the earth is six months later. Then the north pole is tilted away from the sun, and the south pole is tilted toward the sun. Then it is winter north of the equator and summer south of the equator.

1. The earth's orbit is like a road around the sun.

2. The north pole is tilted toward the sun.

3. The earth, six months later

The earth is not a perfect ball. It is flattened a little at the poles, and bulges at the equator. To see why, tie a small ball to a rubber band and swing it around. As the ball swings, a centrifugal force pushes it. This makes the rubber band stretch, allowing the ball to move further away from the center around which it swings. The same sort of thing has happened to the earth. As the earth spins, a centrifugal force tries to push each part of the earth away from the axis. The earth has stretched a little, like a rubber band. The stretching of the earth has allowed the equator to bulge out, away from the axis.

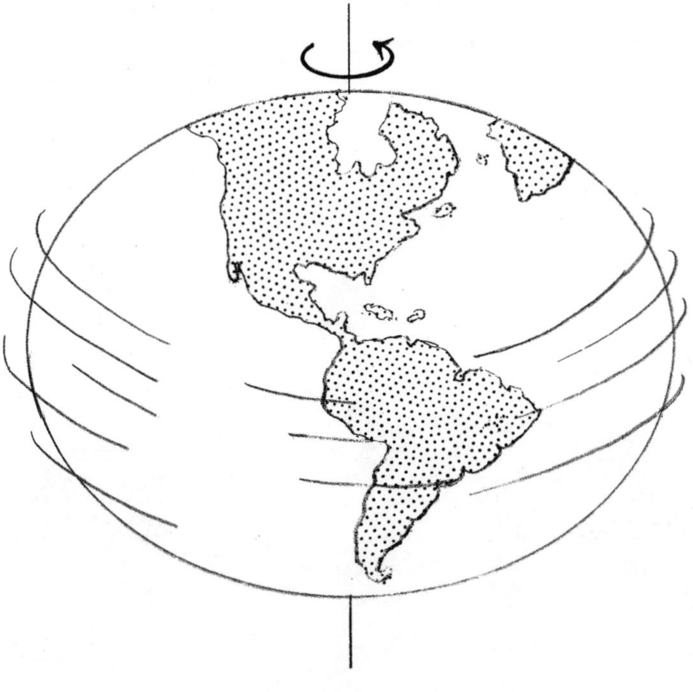

The sun is a great ball far out in space. We have proof that the sun spins like a top, just as the earth does. The proof is seen on pictures of the sun taken through a telescope. These pictures show that there are dark spots on the face of the sun. These spots are storms on the sun. When sun spots appear, they do not stay in one place. They travel in circles around the sun. This shows that the sun is spinning. The sun spins around its axis once in about a month.

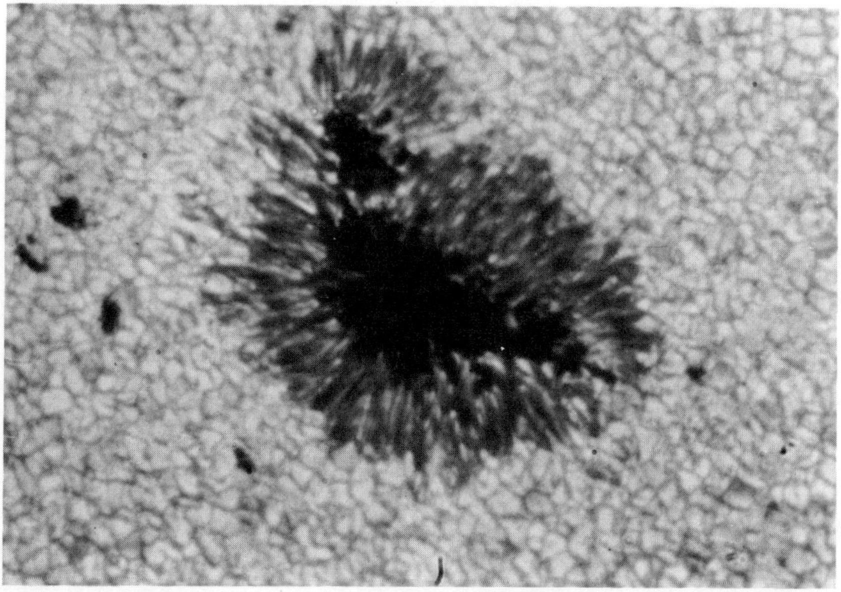

Project Stratoscope. Princeton University

Picture of a sunspot

The moon also spins like a top. Here is proof. *We always see the same side of the moon. The other side is always turned away from us.* But this can happen only if the moon spins. To see why, let a boy and girl play at being earth and moon. Let the boy stand in the middle of the room. He is the earth. Let the girl move around him in a circle. She is the moon. If the girl does not spin, she always faces in the same direction. When she is on one side of the boy, he can see her face. When she is on the other side of him, he can see her back. The boy can

This is what happens if the girl does not spin as she moves around the boy.

This is what happens if the girl spins as she moves around the boy

see her face all the time only if the girl turns slowly as she walks around him. If the moon did not turn, we would see all of the moon. We see the same face of the moon all the time only because the moon turns. The moon turns on its axis once in a month.

In 1959, a rocket fired by Russian scientists made a trip around the moon. A camera in the rocket took a picture of the other side of the moon, and sent it back by radio. This picture gave us our first look at the hidden side of the moon.

In the northern sky there is a group of four bright stars that form the constellation *Andromeda.* The stars are arranged in a line. Near that line is a faint patch of light called the *Great Nebula of Andromeda.* Pictures taken through a big telescope show that the *Great Nebula* is really a giant family of stars. It looks faint only because it is very far away. There are billions of stars in the family. The *Nebula* is shaped like a pin-wheel, with spiral arms. It is spinning around its center, like a pin-wheel blown by the wind. There are many families like this one out in space. They are called *spiral nebulas.* Each one of them is spinning like a top.

Yerkes Observatory

The great nebula in Andromeda

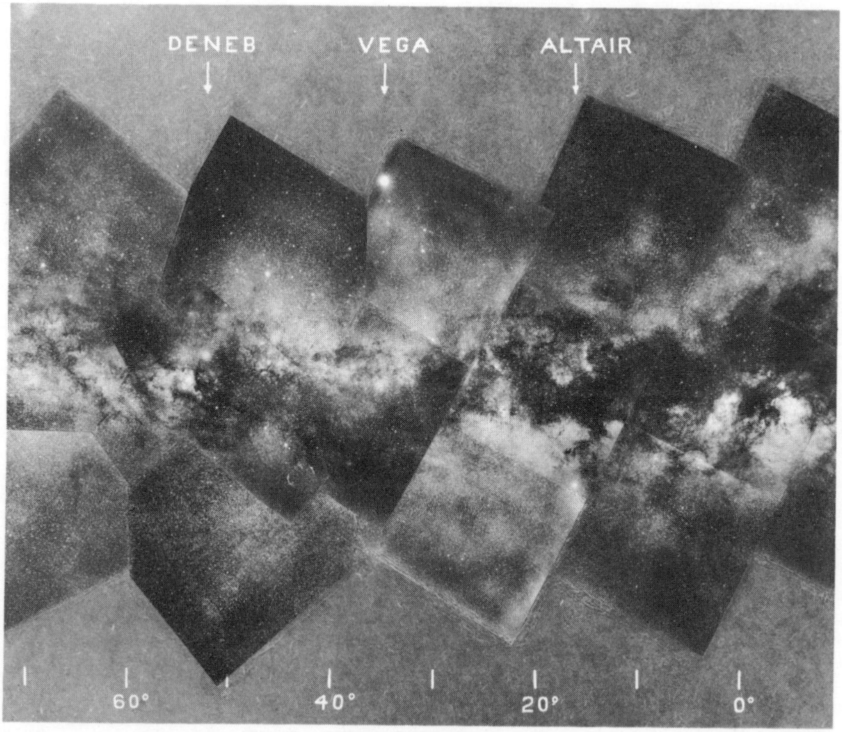

Yerkes Observatory

Part of the Milky Way

The sun and the stars that are nearest to us belong to one of these spiral nebula families. The one we belong to is called the *Galaxy*, or *Milky Way*. It has spiral arms, and it spins like a top. The sun and earth are about half way between the center of the *Galaxy* and its rim. When we look toward the rim, we see many stars crowded together. These crowds of stars form a great circle across the sky. This is how the *Milky Way* looks to us, because we see it from the inside. It is called the *Milky Way* because it is so bright.

Everything in the world is made up of many tiny *atoms*. A single atom is so small that we cannot see it. At the center of an atom is its *nucleus*. *Electrons* surround the nucleus and whirl around it. So each atom is like an invisible top, spinning around its nucleus. The nucleus itself spins, and so does every electron. Every atom, every nucleus, and every electron spins like a top.

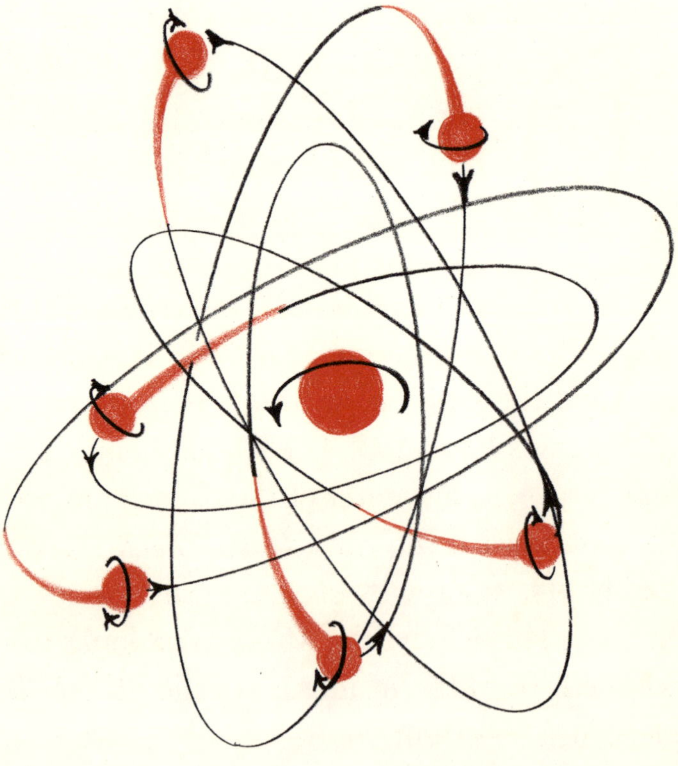

There are spinning tops everywhere. Some of them are toys, like the yo-yo. Some are in machines, like a washing machine. There are tops under us, in us, and around us. The top under us is the earth. The tops that are in us are the atoms, and their nuclei and electrons. The tops around us are the sun, the moon, the stars, and the families of stars called spiral nebulas. When we talk about spinning tops we are really talking about the whole world.

WORD LIST

AXIS — The line around which a top spins.

AUTOMATIC PILOT — An instrument made with gyroscopes, that keeps an airplane flying level and straight.

CENTRIFUGAL FORCE — A force that pushes away from the axis of a spinning top.

FRICTION — The rubbing of one thing against another.

GALAXY — Another name for the Milky Way.

GOVERNOR OF AN ENGINE — Swinging arms that keep the speed of the engine steady.

GYRO-COMPASS — A compass made from a gyroscope whose axis always points north.

GYROSCOPE — A wheel that spins.

GYROSCOPIC STABILIZER — A gyroscope used to keep a ship from rolling.

ORBIT OF THE EARTH — The path the earth follows around the sun.

PENDULUM — A weight swinging at the end of a string or rod.

PRECESSION — The swinging of the axis of a top.

SPIRAL NEBULA — A large family of stars, with arms like a pin-wheel, that spins like a top.